David West ⚇ Children's Books
7 Princeton Court
55 Felsham Road
London SW15 1AZ

Series Concept: Bob Brunning
Designer: Rob Shone
Picture Research: Fiona Thorne
Editor: Ross McLaughness

First published in Great Britain in 2002 by
Heinemann Library, Halley Court, Jordan Hill, Oxford OX2 8EJ, a division of
Reed Educational and Professional Publishing Limited.

OXFORD MELBOURNE AUCKLAND
JOHANNESBURG BLANTYRE GABORONE
IBADAN PORTSMOUTH (NH) USA CHICAGO

World Music

James Pickering

Heinemann
LIBRARY

CONTENTS

INTRODUCTION 5

KING SUNNY ADE 6

BUENA VISTA SOCIAL CLUB 8

THE GIPSY KINGS 10

OFRA HAZA 12

JAJOUKA 14

ANTONIO CARLOS JOBIM 16

NUSRAT FATEH ALI KHAN 18

FELA KUTI 20

LADYSMITH BLACK
MAMBAZO 22

YOUSSOU N'DOUR 24

RAVI SHANKAR 26

ALAN STIVELL 28

GAZETTEER 30

INDEX 32

On these discs is a selection of the artist's recordings. Many of these albums are now available on CD. If they are not, many of the tracks from them can be found on compilation CDs.

These boxes give you extra information about the artists and their times. Some contain anecdotes about the artists themselves or about the people who helped their careers or, occasionally, about those who exploited them. Others provide historical facts about the music, lifestyle, fans, fads and fashions of the day.

The rock star David Byrne (right) has used African and Latin American sounds on his albums.

INTRODUCTION

One of the biggest changes in listening habits over the last few years has been the huge growth in world music. Of course, the expression 'world music' is over-simplistic. All music is world music – where else could it come from?

Like it or not, popular music in the 20th century was largely dominated by North American and British musicians, whose songs can be heard on the radio almost everywhere. Traditional music from other parts of the world (world music) was in danger of dying out as western acts took a stranglehold. But today, world music is alive and well, a massive global industry, and much of its heritage has been preserved.

Sting (above) has also embraced world music. He interrupted his career to concentrate on preserving the Brazilian rainforest. He's pictured here with the native Brazilian Chief Raoni on a tour of the rainforest.

There are several reasons for this revival. Talented individuals, such as Ravi Shankar and Youssou N'Dour, have gained millions of fans through their associations with western rock musicians. Also, people's ears have been opened by the ease of modern travel. Previously inaccessible places are now popular tourist destinations, and music fans often bring home some of the local culture, in CD or cassette form. Simple, modern recording technology has not only preserved world music – it has also enabled it to grow. And world music is not all pipes and drums these days. It's just as likely to be performed using drum machines, synthesizers and electric guitars.

KING SUNNY ADE

Nigeria is a sweltering and often violent republic on Africa's west coast. Today, it has a modern economy based on oil exports, but Nigeria maintains its proud tribal traditions, which stretch back hundreds of years. There are over 250 tribal groups, each with its own culture. 'Juju' music and dance originated in Yoruba, one of the principal African kingdoms.

AFRICAN ARISTOCRAT

Sunday Adeniyi was born into a branch of the royal family of Ondo, a town in the south of the country. He started to play the guitar at an early age and, in 1966, he started his first band, the Green Spots. Changing his name to King Sunny Ade, to highlight his royal connections, he had some success with the Green Spots, and in 1974 he formed his own record label, Sunny Alade. With his eye on the international audience, Ade changed the name of the band to the African Beats and found local fame with the albums 'The Royal Sound' and 'The Late General Murtala Muhammed', a tribute to Nigeria's least unpopular military dictator.

HANDS ACROSS THE WATER

In 1977, Island Records, based in Jamaica, were looking for another tropical star to add to their roster of artists, which included the reggae singer Bob Marley. That year, journalists had named Ade the 'King of Juju Music', and Island were quick to sign him up to a global contract. Juju is a lively music and dance style, almost entirely sung in native languages, mainly Yoruba. It is dominated by driving percussion and joyous vocals, and the guitar line-up of Ade's band, plus his own stage charisma, looked set to win him worldwide stardom. That came with the albums 'Juju Music' and 'Synchro System' in the early 1980s.

'Juju Music' 1982
'Synchro System' 1983
'Live Juju' 1988

'E Dide (Get Up)' 1995
'Odu' 1998
'Seven Degrees North' 2000

King Sunny Ade is known as 'Wizard of the Guitar'.

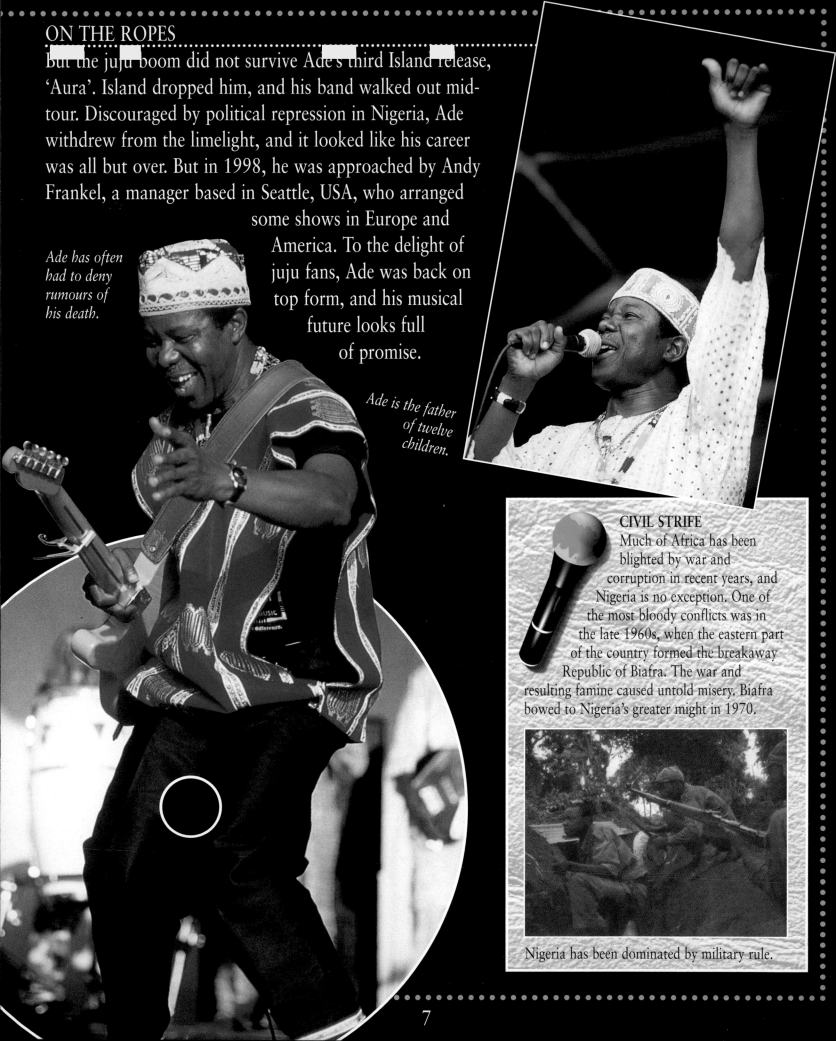

but the juju boom did not survive Ade's third Island release, 'Aura'. Island dropped him, and his band walked out mid-tour. Discouraged by political repression in Nigeria, Ade withdrew from the limelight, and it looked like his career was all but over. But in 1998, he was approached by Andy Frankel, a manager based in Seattle, USA, who arranged some shows in Europe and America. To the delight of juju fans, Ade was back on top form, and his musical future looks full of promise.

Ade has often had to deny rumours of his death.

Ade is the father of twelve children.

CIVIL STRIFE
Much of Africa has been blighted by war and corruption in recent years, and Nigeria is no exception. One of the most bloody conflicts was in the late 1960s, when the eastern part of the country formed the breakaway Republic of Biafra. The war and resulting famine caused untold misery. Biafra bowed to Nigeria's greater might in 1970.

Nigeria has been dominated by military rule.

7

BUENA VISTA SOCIAL CLUB

The American blues guitarist Ry Cooder has successfully collaborated with many international musicians over the years. In 1996, he set out for Cuba, to record traditional 'son' music before it died out.

SAVIOUR OF SON

Son can be played by small acoustic bands or larger and louder brass ensembles. Opening verses are usually followed by improvized phrases from a solo singer and chorus. But until Ry Cooder's intervention, its traditions were in danger of being lost. He brought together for the first time Cuba's most experienced musicians, and recorded them under the name Buena Vista Social Club.

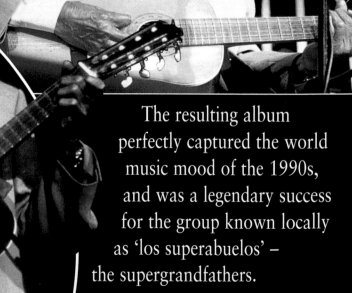

The resulting album perfectly captured the world music mood of the 1990s, and was a legendary success for the group known locally as 'los superabuelos' – the supergrandfathers.

Omara Portuondo (left) provides vocals for the Buena Vista Social Club.

'Buena Vista Social Club' 1997
'Buena Vista Social Club
Presents Ibrahim Ferrer' 1999

'Buena Vista Social Club
Presents Omara Portuondo' 2000

Ry Cooder (below right) has also worked with musicians from India and Mali.

CASTRO'S CUBA

Many people say that the republic of Cuba in the Caribbean is stuck in a time warp. General Fidel Castro led a revolution in 1959, and established a hard-line communist state. This was viewed with deep suspicion by its neighbour, the United States, which imposed trade sanctions. As a result, Cuba has had to fend for itself, rather than rely on imports. 50-year-old cars, like the one below, still cruise the streets, because new ones are mostly unavailable.

General Castro is still in power in the 21st century.

CUBAN OLD TIMERS

The main composer and guitarist Compay Segundo was 89 at the time of the recording. Singer Ibrahim Ferrer, at 70, had not performed for years. The other stars were the pianist Rúben González, 77, and the baby of the band, Eliades Ochoa, who was 49.
The German film-maker Wim Wenders made a documentary about the musicians, which featured archive footage and performances at their sell-out concerts in Amsterdam and New York's prestigious Carnegie Hall.

Ry Cooder produced a solo album by singer Ibrahim Ferrer (below).

NO SIGN OF RETIRING

The group was still playing into the 21st century, though sadly violinist Pedro Depestre Gonzalez collapsed and died on stage in April 2001. But, thanks to Ry Cooder, the music survives.

THE GIPSY KINGS

The wandering Gipsy people of southern France and northern Spain have a legend about how their musical traditions have survived. When an old singer or guitarist is about to die, he will perform in front of a pregnant woman. Her unborn child will then inherit his talent.

KEEPING IT IN THE FAMILY

José Reyes was a famous flamenco singer, who fled Spain for France during the Spanish Civil War in the 1930s. It's not known whether dying musicians played for his wife, but his sons Nicolas, André and Paul formed a group called Los Reyes (the Kings) in the Gipsy areas of Arles and Montpellier, where they grew up. In 1982, they hooked up with their cousins the Baliardos ('guitarists') to form the Gipsy Kings, playing a lively version of 'rumba' music, featuring driving rhythms and rich vocals.

'Volare' was another Gipsy Kings hit.

Nicolas Reyes has a rough-sounding voice.

FAMOUS FRIENDS

The film star Brigitte Bardot is said to have spotted the band busking in St Tropez, and she invited them to perform at a party full of her celebrity friends.

Within months, they had a host of famous fans, including rock guitarist Eric Clapton, and even Princess Diana. With that sort of endorsement, some major concerts were arranged, as well as recording dates.

BAMBOLEO

The pinnacle came with their 1988 self-titled album, which featured the hit single 'Bamboleo'. This song was a must at parties in the late '80s – perhaps it reminded weary listeners of happy holidays in France and Spain. Until the arrival of the Buena Vista Social Club, 'The Gipsy Kings' was the best-selling album of world music to date. Since then, the group has recorded another dozen albums, complete with horns, strings, accordions and even electronic instruments.

FLAMENCO Flamenco music and dance originated on the streets of Spain in about 1750. The music is highly rhythmical and emotional, and dancers need to have immense discipline and poise as they twirl their frilled dresses, revealing agile ankles and feet. Much flamenco dance is improvized to the sound of the accompanying guitar. Dancers hold small wooden castanets between their fingers, which they click vigorously in time to the music. Flamenco has enjoyed a recent surge of publicity, thanks to the popularity of the young dancer Joaquin Cortes.

Flamenco is as popular today as it has ever been.

'The Gipsy Kings' 1988
'Allegria' 1989
'Mosaique' 1989
'Este Mundo' 1991
'Live' 1992

'Love & Liberté' 1994
'Tierra Gitana' 1996
'Compas' 1997
'Cantos De Amor' 1998
'Somos Gitanos' 2001

The Gipsy Kings recorded a version of the Frank Sinatra hit 'My Way' ('A Mi Manera').

OFRA HAZA

Jewish people all over the world have rich traditions of music and culture, none more so than the Yemenite Jews. But Yemen is a Muslim country, and for centuries the Jewish population suffered great persecution, until almost all of them were evacuated to Israel between 1948 and 1950.

'Yemenite Songs' 1985
'Shaday' 1988

'Desert Wind' 1989
'Kirya' 1992

A SAFE HAVEN

Ofra Haza's parents were forced to flee Yemen on foot, and eventually arrived in Tel Aviv. Ofra was born in 1957, and as a child she was steeped in the Yemenite songs which the Jewish people would sing to suit every occasion, at times of celebration and grief, at work and at prayer. In her teens, she joined a theatre group, but her performing career was interrupted by a compulsory two years in the Israeli army. Out of uniform in 1979, she returned to singing and quickly became a star.

VERSATILE STAR

Ofra's local success was not that surprising – Yemenite Jews are amongst the most popular artists in Israel today. What was remarkable was her popularity in neighbouring Arab countries, which have been locked in conflict with Israel for decades. Ofra was a prolific recording artist, and she released a huge body of albums, encompassing styles as varied as disco and goth music. In 1983, she was chosen to represent her country in the Eurovision Song Contest.

Ofra's songs were turned into dance tracks by club DJs.

YEMENITE SONGS

Ofra returned to her musical roots with 'Yemenite Songs', which was inspired by the age-old melodies she had learned from her mother. The songs are accompanied by the clattering of metal – the Jews in Yemen had been forbidden musical instruments and played on oil drums and trays instead. Ofra's dignified, pure and velvety voice turned the album into a triumphant success. Tragically, her career was cut short by her early and unexpected death in February 2000.

PROTEST MUSIC

Despite the ban on instruments, the Yemenite Jews still managed to preserve their musical heritage. All over the world, oppressive regimes have tried to stifle the traditions of minority peoples. The aboriginal peoples of Australia suffered harsh treatment under European settlers, but many of their survival skills, languages and legends are being rediscovered. Aboriginal ceremonial dances, or 'corroborees' are popular tourist attractions all over Australia these days.

Aboriginals blow through a long wooden pipe called a didgeridoo.

Ofra died from an AIDS-related disease.

JAJOUKA

The foothills of the Rif mountains in Morocco are home to the Berber people. Despite its proud history, this Muslim race and its music were virtually unknown in the West until a few years ago.

MUSICAL BROTHERHOOD

The Master Musicians Of Jajouka are Berber musicians who have been playing for generations. The Master Musicians make up a close brotherhood, the leadership of which is passed down from father to son – the present leader, Bachir Attar, inherited the title when his father died in 1982. They produce 'trance music', a hypnotic mixture of driving rhythms on double-headed drums, and the droning sound of the 'ghaita', a double-reed pipe, similar to the oboe.

EAST MEETS WEST

The Moroccan city of Tangier was a haven for artists, actors and writers in the 1960s. In 1968, several members of the rock group the Rolling Stones paid a visit, and their guitarist Brian Jones was intrigued to meet the Master Musicians, who had never been heard in the West. Jones made a number of simple recordings of the group, and mixed the tapes on his return to London, adding all sorts of electronic special effects.

A rare colour photograph of the Master Musicians in about 1911.

CONTINENTAL DRIFT

Brian Jones died before the results were released, but the Rolling Stones issued the album as a tribute to him in 1971. For many years, this was the only record of Moroccan music available in the West. Nevertheless, the Master Musicians remained in relative obscurity until the Stones paid another visit in 1989. The Master Musicians contributed to the song 'Continental Drift' which opened concerts on the Stones' next massive world tour.

FAME AT LAST

Since then, the Master Musicians have recorded CDs, and have played at important festivals all over the world. There have been reports of bad blood with another band, who also claim to be the Master Musicians. But Bachir Attar's Master Musicians Of Jajouka are true ambassadors for the Berber people.

WORLDLY ROCK MUSICIANS

Brian Jones (right) helped to open western ears to world music, when it was usually only heard in foreign films or in restaurants. Perhaps Jones was influenced by George Harrison, who had introduced Indian sounds on the Beatles' records. Other rock musicians who have embraced world music are Peter Gabriel, who founded the Real World label, and David Byrne, who has championed African and South American music on his Luaka Bop label.

Brian Jones

Joujouka

Brian Jones was a multi-instrumentalist, who played the Indian sitar and African marimba.

'Brian Jones Presents The Pipes Of Pan At Jajouka'
1971
'Apocalypse Across The Sky'
1992

'Jajouka Between The Mountains'
1996
'Master Musicians Of Jajouka'
2000

The Master Musicians play Moroccan drums, the 'ghaita' and the 'lira', a bamboo flute.

Bachir Attar (left) plays the 'guimbri', a three-stringed instrument.

ANTONIO CARLOS JOBIM

What's the latest craze this year? Perhaps a new hip-hop act has taken the charts by storm, or a boy band has invented a new dance routine. Back in the late 1950s, the coolest sound on the radio was 'bossa nova', a gentle style of music, originally based around a singer and solo guitar. It emerged from the vast South American country of Brazil, and it was the invention of one man, Antonio Carlos Jobim.

BIRTH OF BOSSA NOVA

It's very rare that a single person can take the credit for coming up with a new musical style, but Antonio certainly deserved to be called the father of bossa nova. The coastal city of Rio de Janeiro has always been the musical capital of Brazil. It was the birthplace of 'samba', an energetic and highly rhythmical accompaniment to the Rio Carnaval, a huge street party which takes over the city every year. Antonio was a classically trained guitarist, who liked to spend time in the chic beach neighbourhood of Ipanema during the day and in Rio's lively bars and clubs at night. His idea was to develop relaxed, laid-back, but samba-based music. Bossa nova was born.

Antonio Carlos Jobim's nickname was Tom.

CARNAVAL

All countries colonized by Catholics have celebrations in the days leading up to Ash Wednesday, the first day of Lent, but Brazil goes a lot further. The entire country shuts down for five days from the previous Friday, and almost everybody joins in the biggest party in the world. Each year, the Carnaval songs have to be new, so during the previous weeks, music fills the airwaves, as dozens of musicians compete to create that year's biggest Carnaval hit.

OUT OF TUNE

The first bossa nova record was called 'Desafinado', which means 'out of tune'. Penned by Antonio, and sung by João Gilberto, it was an instant smash in 1957. João's wife Astrud sang an English version of Antonio's 'The Girl From Ipanema', which became Brazil's biggest ever international hit. By now, bossa nova was being embraced by famous American jazz musicians, such as Stan Getz, as the ultimate in smooth musical sophistication.

'The Man From Ipanema' 1963
'Wave' 1967
'Urubu' 1976

'Terra Brasilis' 1980
'Live At The Free Jazz Festival' 1993
'Antonio Brasileiro' 1995

Samba music came out of the Carnaval.

Antonio died in 1996, aged 67.

BORN AGAIN

Like all crazes, bossa nova had a limited lifespan, and it could not survive the rock and pop explosion of the 1960s. But in Brazil, it lived on, and Antonio became a highly respected figure on the local pop music scene. Bossa nova has enjoyed a recent revival in New York clubs, where the Brazilian producer Arto Lindsay has mixed drum 'n' bass rhythms with the bossa nova singing of Vinicius Cantuária.

NUSRAT FATEH ALI KHAN

The Sufi Muslim people of Pakistan believe that music has spiritual qualities, which can transport the performer and listener closer to God. 'Qawwali' is the Sufi music of love and peace, which has traditions stretching back 800 years. Its singers are called 'qawwals', and Nusrat Fateh Ali Khan was the most famous qawwal who has ever lived.

MUSICAL DYNASTY

Nusrat was born in Faisalabad in 1948, into a family which has produced qawwali singers for six centuries – his father was a well-known classical musician and qawwal. Groups of qawwals are varied, and can consist of any number of people, but are always based around a lead singer, one or two backing singers, who also play the harmonium, and a percussionist. Every group member joins in the singing, accompanied by fierce clapping. In a traditional performance, the qawwal repeats lyrics about holy love over and over again, and Nusrat could make his shrill voice soar over the accompanists. Even Nusrat's western audiences, who were unaware of the spiritual meaning of qawwali, could be mesmerized by the sheer power and beauty of his voice.

Nusrat recorded for Peter Gabriel's Real World label.

'Musst Musst' 1990
'Shahbaaz' 1991
'Devotional Songs' 1993

'Night Song' 1996
'Star Rise' 1998
'Final Studio Recordings' 2001

SOUNDTRACKER

Nusrat was already a superstar on the Indian subcontinent when the English rock star Peter Gabriel invited him to sing on the soundtrack of the film 'The Last Temptation Of Christ'. Sufi is a tolerant branch of Islam, and although he was a devout man, Nusrat was willing to explore other cultures. He went on to appear on several more soundtracks, including that to the violent American movie 'Natural Born Killers'. Qawwali is very accessible to western ears, and lends itself easily to dance remixes. Nitin Sawhney, Joi and Asian Dub Foundation remixed Nusrat's music for the album 'Star Rise', a club hit in 1997.

Talvin Singh (above) has remixed Nusrat's music.

BHANGRA

The style of music called 'bhangra' started out as a folk dance, which celebrated the harvest in the Punjab region over 200 years ago. Led by the 'dhol', a loud wooden drum, bhangra can easily be adapted to fit electronic dance rhythms, particularly house and hip-hop beats. Today, Britain is a multicultural society, and bhangra raves were popular in London and the Midlands throughout the 1980s and '90s.

Cornershop (above) is one of the most popular bhangra groups.

MASSIVE HIT

The dance/rap outfit Massive Attack remixed the title track from Nusrat's 'Musst Musst' album, and it turned into an international hit when Coca Cola used it in a TV commercial. If it seemed strange that this deeply religious music should be used to advertise a soft drink, then Nusrat didn't mind. His job as a qawwal was to move as many people as possible closer to God, and millions of people watch TV!

Nusrat Fateh Ali Khan died in 1997.

FELA KUTI

Along with King Sunny Ade, Fela Kuti was one of the most important artists to emerge from West Africa. Like Ade, Fela was born into the Yoruba tribe of Nigeria, and he invented Afro-beat, a heady mixture of thunderous percussion and brass, and vocals sung in pidgin, a simple type of English. Fela's politics won him few friends amongst the Nigerian authorities.

Fela was often photographed without his shirt!

UNLIKELY DOCTOR

Fela was born in 1938, the son of a Protestant minister who hoped that his son would become a doctor. Instead, Fela travelled to London's Trinity College of Music, where he studied trumpet, and started his first band, Koola Lobitos, in 1961. During a trip to the USA, Fela fell in with the militant civil rights campaigners, the Black Panthers, and was deeply influenced by American jazz and funk music. Back home, he blended these styles with African music in his huge Afro-beat band Africa 70, which included 20 female dancers and singers.

'Teacher Don't Teach Me Nonsense' 1987
'The Best Best Of Fela Kuti' 1999
'Coffin For Head Of State' 2000

'Shuffering And Shmiling' 2000
'Monkey Banana' 2001
'Zombie' 2001

A BRAVE MUSICIAN

Fela's records often attacked the incompetence and corruption of the Nigerian regime. His wit and satire appealed to ordinary people, but he was constantly hounded by the government. In 1977, about 1,000 soldiers attacked and burnt his home, and threw his 82-year-old mother out of a window. But Fela refused to change his ideas, and continued to taunt the authorities with his music.

BANGED UP

In 1984, Fela was sent to prison on a false smuggling charge. In typically eccentric fashion, Fela divorced all 28 of his wives on the same day, while he was inside. Worldwide protest eventually helped to secure his release in 1987, and he returned triumphantly with a new band, Egypt 80, and yet more protest records. But in the '90s, Fela's hard lifestyle was catching up with him. He died in 1997, from an AIDS-related illness. To the disgust of the authorities, around a million mourners attended his funeral.

Fela switched from trumpet to tenor saxophone.

KUTI JUNIOR

Fela Kuti's son, Femi, has enjoyed a successful career since the late 1980s, with his group the Positive Force. The Nigerian people have taken Femi to their hearts, especially since his father's death. Femi Kuti is recognizably his father's son in his voice, lyrics and muscular physique. And like his father, he only wears clothes when strictly necessary!

Femi Kuti is signed to the large Polygram label.

Fela Kuti sang in pidgin, which is used by merchants who don't speak the same language.

LADYSMITH BLACK MAMBAZO

Like Nusrat Fateh Ali Khan, Ladysmith Black Mambazo enjoyed unexpected success courtesy of a TV commercial, in their case for baked beans! The catchy 'Inkanyezi Nezazi' reached the top 20 in 1997, but the group's international fame goes back a lot further than that.

'Ulwandle Oluncgwele' 1985
'Shaka Zulu' 1988
'Two Worlds One Heart' 1991

'Gift Of The Tortoise' 1994
'Liph' Iquiniso' 1994
'Live At The Royal Albert Hall' 1999

MUSIC TO TIPTOE TO

Ladysmith Black Mambazo is a South African Zulu choir, which sings in soft harmonies called 'iscathamiya'. This Zulu word means to 'step softly'. When Zulu men left their villages to work in factories and mines, they stayed in all-male hostels, where rowdy singing and stomping were unwelcome, so they developed a quiet song and dance style.

CUT OFF FROM THE WORLD

The group was formed by Joseph Shabalala in the early 1960s, in the town of Ladysmith. The line-up has changed over the years, but has always been based around three families – four of Joseph's sons are current members. 'Mambazo' means 'axe', because the group boasted that they cut down all their rivals in early singing competitions. Their first album, 'Amabutho', was released in 1973, but South Africa was ruled by an apartheid system in those days – black people and those of mixed race were denied basic rights by the white minority. As a result, many nations imposed trade and cultural sanctions against South Africa, and Zulu music was rarely heard in the West. All that changed in 1986, when the rock musician Paul Simon ignored the ban, and recorded in South Africa.

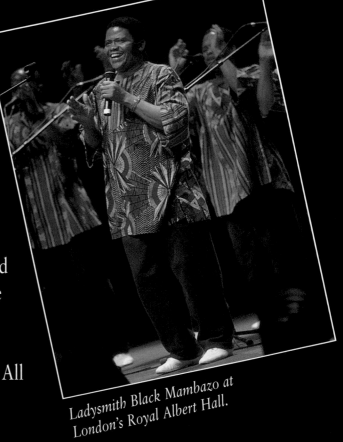

Ladysmith Black Mambazo at London's Royal Albert Hall.

A clenched fist is a symbol of black power.

GRACELAND

Paul Simon argued that the cultural ban was stifling the very people it was meant to help. His album 'Graceland', featuring Ladysmith Black Mambazo, was an enormous hit, and he took them on tour around the world. It was the first time the choir had sung to racially mixed audiences. In 1988, he produced the group's award-winning album 'Shaka Zulu'. Since then, Ladysmith Black Mambazo has collaborated with many western musicians, including Des'ree and the Lighthouse Family. But the group is at its best singing the pure and soft harmonies of the proud Zulu people.

APARTHEID

Under apartheid, black South Africans were not allowed to vote, enter parliament, go on to white beaches, and white and black children were educated in separate schools. Nelson Mandela fought against the South African government and its racist policies. He was imprisoned for political offences in 1964, and became a symbol of black resistance. South Africa finally reformed its government in the early 1990s, and Nelson Mandela went on to become his country's first black President.

Nelson Mandela on his release from prison in 1990.

The group's harmonies are both complex and uplifting.

YOUSSOU N'DOUR

Music is a vital part of everyday life in West Africa. Everywhere children imitate the dancing and drumming of their elders, while women sing work songs to the rhythm of pounding pestles and mortars. Professional musicians are a vital part of religious ceremonies. In the past this role was reserved for those born into the 'griot' caste.

Youssou recorded 'In Your Eyes' with Peter Gabriel.

EVER THE GRIOT

Youssou N'Dour is the son of a mechanic, and he received little formal education when he was growing up in the small country of Senegal. But Youssou was born into the griot caste, and took his duties very seriously from a young age, learning by heart a vast repertoire of traditional songs. To this day, Youssou considers himself a griot, singing songs which offer religious advice and warnings. Although griots are admired and sometimes held in awe by their fellow citizens, they do not rank highly on the social scale, and this partly explains Youssou's huge popularity amongst the ordinary people of Senegal. He started his first band, Etoile de Dakar in 1979, playing rhythmic 'mbalax' music, with a Cuban-style brass section.

LIVE ATTRACTION

Youssou attracted the attention of the English rock star Peter Gabriel, who helped him to land a contract with Virgin Records. Youssou also joined Gabriel, Bruce Springsteen and Sting on the 1988 'Human Rights Now!' charity tour, and was given a rousing welcome by western rock fans. But despite his live reputation, Youssou's records failed to sell in large quantities, and Virgin dropped him after two albums.

MAN OF THE PEOPLE

Youssou's fortunes took an upturn in 1994, when he signed with Sony. His single '7 Seconds' was one of the biggest pop hits of the year, and it propelled his album 'The Guide' to global success. Today Youssou is the biggest star of African music, and even listeners with no particular interest in world music know his name. But Youssou remains true to his roots – he produces at least two albums for the Senegalese market each year and has built recording facilities to promote African music independently from large western record companies. Youssou also keeps his loyal fans happy by performing each week at a small club in Dakar. Can you imagine a western rock star doing the same?

Youssou created the Jololi label to promote African music.

'The Lion' 1989
'Set' 1990
'Eyes Open' 1992
'The Guide (Wommat)' 1994

'Grand Bal' 2000
'Joko' 2000
'Lii!' 2000
'Birth Of A Star' 2001

BAABA MAAL

Youssou N'Dour only has one rival for the title of Senegal's biggest musical star – Baaba Maal. In fact, their styles are very different. While Youssou lives in the capital Dakar, Baaba comes from the remote north of the country, on the fringes of the vast Sahara desert. His music is influenced by the Islamic nomads who inhabit this inhospitable area. On his 1998 album, 'Nomad Soul' Baaba collaborated with western stars Brian Eno and Sinéad O'Connor.

Baaba Maal performed for the South African statesman Nelson Mandela in 2001.

RAVI SHANKAR

One man has done more than anyone to popularize not just Indian music, but all world music – Ravi Shankar. Even before the expression 'world music' had been invented, Ravi was enchanting western listeners with his sensitive and virtuoso mastery of the sitar, one of the most difficult instruments to learn anywhere in the world.

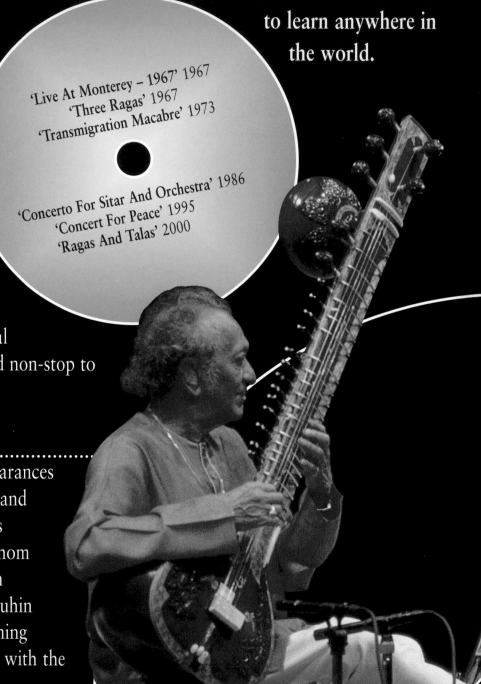

'Live At Monterey – 1967' 1967
'Three Ragas' 1967
'Transmigration Macabre' 1973

'Concerto For Sitar And Orchestra' 1986
'Concert For Peace' 1995
'Ragas And Talas' 2000

SITAR HERO

The sitar is a long-necked instrument, similar to the guitar, but with two sets of finely-tuned strings, played in a cross-legged position. Ravi Shankar was born in the province of Uttar Pradesh, close to India's modern capital city, New Delhi, in 1920. He showed early promise on the sitar – he gave his first professional performance at the age of 13, and studied non-stop to develop his skills.

WESTERN FRIENDS

Ravi Shankar made his first concert appearances in Europe and America in the late 1950s and early '60s. These shows had an enormous impact on western musicians, many of whom knew little of the rich traditions of Indian classical music. The violinist Yehudi Menuhin collaborated with Ravi on an award-winning album in 1966, but it was his association with the Beatles that won him worldwide fame.

A NEW GENERATION OF FANS

The Beatles were the biggest pop group in the world when their guitarist George Harrison tuned into Indian music. Ravi gave George strict lessons, not just about sitar technique, but about respect for the instrument and its traditions. The Beatles' track 'Norwegian Wood' was the first use of sitar in a pop song. Ravi wowed hippy fans with his performance at the 1967 Monterey Pop Festival, and opened a star line-up at the benefit concerts for the suffering people of Bangladesh in 1971. Ravi Shankar spent the next 30 years touring the world, proving himself to be arguably the finest musician on the planet.

Ravi recorded 'West Meets East' with Yehudi Menuhin (below left).

Ravi Shankar on stage with his daughter Anoushka.

POINTS EAST

World music doesn't stop at India – it goes even further East than that. The traditional music of eastern Russia, Siberia, China and Japan still thrives, even though those countries are yet to give the world superstars like those from India, Africa, South America and the Middle East. Japan has given us 'enka', often compared to American soul music, as well as folk, classical and noisy rock music. In China, the traditional music is usually based around simple wind and percussion instruments, which have been played for centuries.

In Tuva, southern Siberia, Sailyk Ommun and Yat-Kha blend traditional and rock music.

George Harrison (below) described Ravi Shankar as the 'godfather of world music'.

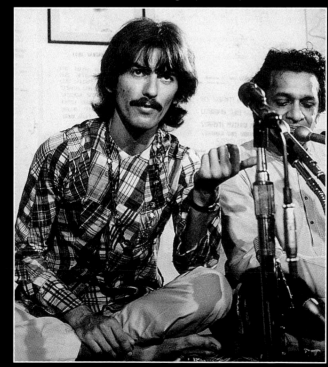

ALAN STIVELL

Today Celtic people live all over the world. From New York to New Zealand, the descendents of Irish, Scottish, Welsh, Cornish and Breton people cling proudly to their traditions. But one part of Celtic heritage nearly died out a few years ago – the Breton harp, from Brittany in north western France.

HARP WORK

Alan Stivell is a true star, who played a major role in the invention of folk-rock music in the 1970s, and put traditional Breton and Celtic music in the charts. But his greatest achievement was to pull the Breton harp back from the brink of extinction, and revive a unique part of Celtic heritage. But Alan was not working alone – he was carrying on the work of his father.

Alan's harp accompanies his singing.

FOLLOWING IN FATHER'S FOOTSTEPS

Alan Cochevelou was born in Brittany, the son of a harp-maker. Alan's father had rediscovered the Breton harp, but his efforts at promoting the instrument went largely ignored. It was only when Alan started performing at the age of eleven that people began to take notice of this endangered instrument. In his teens, Alan studied all aspects of Celtic music, including the Irish flute, tin whistle and the bagpipes, for which he won awards in Scottish national championships.

'Renaissance Of The Celtic Harp' 1972
'Journée A La Maison' 1978
'Celtic Symphony' 1979
'Harpes Du Nouvel Age' 1986

'The Mist Of Avalon' 1991
'Zoom' 1997
'1 Douar' 1998
'Back To Breizh' 2000

SOURCE OF INSPIRATION

During the 1960▮, Alan changed his surname to Stivell, the Breton word for 'fountain', or 'spring'. In 1972, he released the classic album 'Renaissance Of The Celtic Harp' which prompted hundreds of players to take up the instrument, where 20 years before there had been none. Alan has also mastered harps from Ireland, Scotland and Wales on his albums, and has collaborated with rock musicians, such as Kate Bush. The Celtic harp is alive and well once more, its hauntingly beautiful sound preserved forever on CD – and all thanks to Alan Stivell.

EASTERN EUROPE

The Celtic music of Alan Stivell originates from the most westerly points of Europe. Far in the east of Europe the musical traditions are just as rich. 'La Mystère Des Voix Bulgares' is one of the most successful recent albums of European music. The record started a wave of interest in Bulgarian music, in particular the intricate harmonies and arrangements sung by choirs of female singers, who have a vocal range of just one octave. In total, the ensemble has released four albums of its unique music.

'La Mystère Des Voix Bulgares' has been performed all over the world.

Celtic music is often improvized at informal gatherings called ceilidhs.

GAZETTEER

By its very nature, world music is a global phenomenon. Of course, in a book of this size there isn't room to examine in detail every recording artist, or style of music, but the following have all made a major contribution to the music of the world.

Caetano Veloso also paints, writes poetry and directs his own videos.

Ricky Martin is a huge star in the USA.

MUSIC FROM THE TROPICS

Caetano Veloso has been at the forefront of Brazilian music for over 40 years. He sings in the 'tropicalismo' style, as does Gilberto Gil, who spent many years in London because of his opposition to the Brazilian military regime.

The Afro-Celt Sound System combines Irish folk music with techno in their live act.

Tito Puente died in Puerto Rico in 1973.

Gilberto Gil is influenced by reggae and rock music.

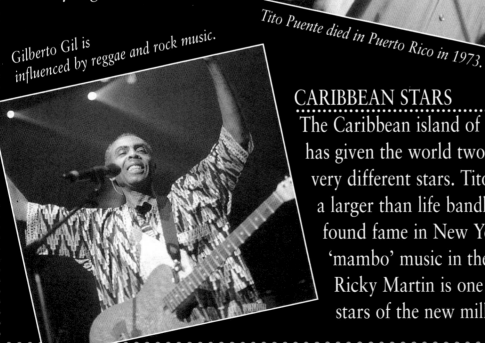

CARIBBEAN STARS

The Caribbean island of Puerto Rico has given the world two huge, but very different stars. Tito Puente was a larger than life bandleader, who found fame in New York, playing 'mambo' music in the 1950s.
Ricky Martin is one of the biggest stars of the new millennium.

The Mighty Sparrow has recorded over 100 albums.

Ricky
has blended the 'salsa' music
of the island with pure pop, and won himself
millions of fans. The Mighty Sparrow from nearby Trinidad
is a popular figure throughout the Caribbean. His witty
songs sum up the 'calypso' style.

SOUNDS OF AFRICA

Salif Keita comes from Mali, a huge landlocked country in western
Africa. He overcame poor eyesight and the social stigma of being born
with white skin to become Mali's most popular singer. Further north in
Algeria, Khaled is the superstar of 'rai'
singing. He has enjoyed astounding success
at home, in France and, perhaps surprisingly,
in India.

UNIQUE MIXTURE

The Afro-Celt Sound System surprised
many people with their unlikely blend of
West African and Celtic instruments, with
electronic dance beats thrown in. Their
records and live shows have been a huge
success since 1996, a fine example of
different cultures coming together to create
something new and exciting.

Khaled started his career under the name Cheb Khaled.

Salif Keita's noble family opposed his choice of career.